Mennonite Education: Why and How?

A Philosophy of Education for the Mennonite Church

By Daniel Hertzler

In collaboration with
Don Augsburger
Paul Bender
Ira E. Miller
Laban Peachey
John H. Yoder

HERALD PRESS
SCOTTDALE, PENNSYLVANIA

MENNONITE EDUCATION: WHY AND HOW?
Copyright © 1971 by Herald Press, Scottdale, Pa. 15683
Library of Congress Catalog Card Number: 73-172267
International Standard Book Number: 0-8361-1655-0
Printed in the United States

Foreword

The document which follows is the work of a committee. We do not apologize for this, but it seems proper to call it to the attention of the reader. As described in Appendix B, the Philosophy of Christian Education Study Committee is ultimately responsible for this statement of educational philosophy.

But a committee as a whole can scarcely research and write, so the work was assigned to a Research Committee, who employed six researchers and also constrained the chairman to do certain investigations and to draft and — as it developed — to redraft the report.

What follows is thus the result of the efforts of many persons. Names of the Study and Research Committees are given in Appendix B along with several additional persons who participated in the study process. Those who have worked most intensively on this document are the members of the Research Committee, whose names appear on the title page. In addition there are the members of the Study Committee plus additional interested and concerned persons.

Thanks are due Albert J. Meyer, Executive Secretary of the Mennonite Board of Education, for personal interest in the project and for patient, probing, questioning counsel to the writer, and to Ben Cutrell, Publisher, Mennonite Publishing House, for approving the writing time which went into the project.

A variety of reactions has come from persons who examined early copies of this document. Some were puzzled, others disappointed, and other reactions might be roughly translated "So what?" As an attempt to help introduce the reader gently, the following "Notes to the Reader in a Hurry" was added.

Beyond this it may be mentioned that this is a very broad outline and begins a great many topics which are not finished. If the outline can be accepted as valid, each reader may use it as foundation on which to build additional structure in his specific area.

June 15, 1971
Daniel Hertzler, Chairman
Philosophy of Christian Education
Research Committee

Notes
to the Reader in a Hurry

1. **If at all possible don't hurry.** We think that just about all we have written is important, for of course that is why we have included it. To understand what we are trying to say, we urge a thoughtful step-by-step pilgrimage through the whole.

2. **If haste is necessary, begin with Chapter 3.** This is the heart of the document. It provides our proposed answers to a series of basic educational questions: the questions of educational purposes (Why?), educational process (What?), educational settings (Where?) and learning theories and educational philosophies (How?).

3. **Our too brief answers to these questions are as follows:**

   a. *The purposes of education* include helping learners find out who they are and how they relate to others, and preparing them for service. Church educators are also concerned about two other somewhat contrasting educational tasks: (a) to educate their own people to live as Christians in spite of the influences of the larger society; (b) to provide education as a service to persons in need of it as an opportunity for Christain witness.

   b. *At least four elements* are provided by an adequate educational program. They are: (a) giving information and perspective on the stream of people of which the learners are a part; (b) teaching of values; (c) training in skills; (d) helping each learner come to a view of reality that is significant for him. More than one of these may be going on at the same time and it is hard to separate them into neat categories. But we believe that anyone concerned about a whole educational program needs to keep them all in mind.

c. *Church education is best done in community.* By "community" we mean a group small enough for people to know each other and interact on a personal basis. No educational program which reduces students to ciphers is adequate. In fact, there is a specific limit on the number of learners who can relate to each other meaningfully. We believe this limit should be respected.

d. *We lack the knowledge* to make final statements about some aspects of education. The field of learning theories is an example of this problem. Our attitude toward other current philosophies of education is another. We have some cautious statements about the usefulness of various theories, but we recognize the need for much more study and experimentation.

4. Do-it-yourself strategy. The ten-point educational strategy outlined in Chapter 4 is intended as an expression of the basic philosophy in Chapter 3. It does not go far enough, but we hope it suggests directions which if followed can lead to where the church ought to go educationally.

5. Appendix A is basic. The foundation of our philosophy study is the set of "Theological Statements" which appear as Appendix A. Read them first if you really want to start at the beginning. They were developed in consultation with Mennonite theological thinkers and we believe they can be useful as a setting for the Mennonite educational thinking and practice.

6. Our point of view. We view the church as the people of God, called to be somewhat apart from any other people. Though not at home anywhere, they are at the same time at home everywhere, for their identity and membership cut across all manmade boundaries. This special calling is both a privilege and a responsibility. Because their ultimate goals and manner of life will be different from others, the people of God have specific educational needs and problems. The document which follows is an attempt to write a philosophy of education for people of God.

7. A modest effort. Our use of the name "Mennonite" is not intended as denominational snobbery. Rather it is an attempt to apply a vision of the church and our understanding of what it is to be Christian to the educational problems Christians face in our day. Given our assumptions as outlined in Appendix A and the further information of the research in back of this project, we see purposes and methods of education described here as significant for people such as we are. We assume that other Christian groups with these same assumptions will have many of the same concerns.

8. What kind of education: This document refers more often to education or church education than to "Christian" education. This is to allow for the broadest possible application of these principles. Christian education is sometimes defined narrowly as mainly Bible teaching. We are concerned about all educational work done in the name of the church and for the purposes described on the following pages.

Contents

1

Introduction:

How Have We Come Here?

I have tried in my time to be a philosopher but cheerfulness was always breaking in. — *Oliver Edwards*

Philosophical questions about identity, purpose, or method are second-level questions. That is, they are at least one step beyond the level of bare existence. Or to look at it another way, they are asked by people who are able or forced to step back from actual experience and ponder its meaning.

It is not necessary to be gloomy to be a philosopher, but it sometimes helps. The new couple on their honeymoon or the proprietor of Joe's Fruit Stand in the busy season have no time for philosophical questions. These are reserved for the times when the realities of business or married life press the partners in any enterprise to ask themselves the ultimate questions: Who are we? Should we do this? and, If so, how is it best accomplished?

In education, too, there are times when every effort must be poured into tasks immediately at hand. There are teachers to hire, students to enroll, buildings to build, all these and more at the same time. At other times we need to pause long enough to ask ourselves what we are really trying to accomplish — to ask the basic questions of this report: Why and How?

North American Mennonite education was not without educational philosophers in the early years of the twentieth century.

11

But the Mennonite Church had difficulty translating its heritage into educational philosophy. In addition, the philosophical thinking was done mainly by persons working on philosophy for specific levels of teaching.[1]

It would be too much to say that Mennonites had a honeymoon with education. From the beginning of the Mennonite Sunday school movement in the nineteenth century, there were both those who favored and those who opposed the church's educational efforts. But soon after 1960 it became apparent to some that a new situation had developed.

Opposition to education as such had nearly disappeared. In its place had come so much education and so many institutions that their adequate support seemed threatened. New schools were being organized and proposed while some of those already in existence did not feel adequately supported. In addition there was a lack of coordination of program among various groups concerned about the education of the same persons.

So an early concern was to ask how Mennonite dollars and personnel should be used in doing the educational work that the church needed to be doing. "We need a depth study of the philosophy of education," reads a minute from a meeting of Mennonite higher educational administrators in the early sixties. "Our study should become an instrument of the church to sharpen her conscience on her responsibility . . . we need to sensitize our constituency to the importance of higher education in the brotherhood."

This concern eventually broadened to include interest in a denominational philosophy which could be related to the educational work of the church on all levels. In 1964 the Mennonite Board of Education spoke to the question by asking the Higher Education Council to accept the "initiative in setting up an organization to formulate a philosophy of education for education in Mennonite schools."[2]

The committee which met first on March 5, 1966, has been known as the Philosophy of Christian Education Study Committee. It represents the Mennonite Board of Education and the schools of the Mennonite Church, the Mennonite Commission for Chris-

12

tian Education which guides the work of congregational education, the Mennonite Publishing House and two mission-service agencies, Mennonite Board of Missions and Charities and Eastern Mennonite Board of Missions and Charities.

This committee has functioned mainly through its subcommittee, the Philosophy of Christian Education Research Committee. This subcommittee was asked to carry out the investigations needed and to draft a philosophy of education for the Mennonite Church. The names of the members of these committees and a brief chronology of the study process are given in Appendix B.

The present document is both a report of this research committee to its parent body and an effort to engage in conversation with those seeking answers to the basic questions of Mennonite educational philosophy, questions which may be summarized briefly as three: Why do we educate? Whom do we educate? and How? Or even more succinctly, "Mennonite Education — Why and How?"

Four problems of philosophy concerned the Study Committee as they gave us our assignment. They wished us to study: (1) a theology to inform church education; (2) the educational development of persons in light of our theology; (3) the implications of these findings for education in the home, congregation, and school; (4) finding ways to have these implications put into practice by the church.[3] This report is intended to speak to the first three. Having the ideas accepted and put into practice by the church requires a process of presentation and discussion with various groups responsible for Mennonite education.

As the research committee prepared to put the study process in motion, we clarified for ourselves the definition of "philosophy" which we would use. We agreed that for us it should mean more than abstract questions of reality, truth, and value. Rather we are seeking some means by which to project goals and measure the quality of the educational process: "a tool whereby educators can guide what they do, and test what they have done in the light of what the churches asked them to do."[4]

A philosophy, however, must have a foundation. With our commitment to the Christian faith it was clear that we should begin with theology. So the first step was to have prepared a

13

series of theological statements as a summary of the biblical faith on which to build our philosophical system. This set of statements not only served to guide our philosophical investigations, but itself became a basis for theological discussion among Mennonites. Thus the original draft was expanded and revised through several stages and now appears as Appendix A to this report.

But because for us the theology came first, both in time and in emphasis, we begin our report with a brief statement of the theology which guided our study.

This theological preface is followed by our two main chapters and an epilogue. The first of these three is a discussion of basic philosophical questions with our proposed answers. The second is a proposed ten-point strategy for Mennonite education and the last is an attempt to summarize and to bring the report to a smooth ending.

2

Theological Preface

Education is not done in a vacuum. Every Sunday school teacher has certain assumptions on which to base his efforts. Even the teacher who is concerned more about job security than learning must certainly give occasional thought to what he is doing and why.

The decision to use a theological base for our statement of philosophy not only helps to protect us from overdependence on unexamined classical or current systems of philosophy. It bases our philosophy firmly on the biblical faith.

The reader is encouraged to refer regularly to Appendix A for help in understanding the theological assumptions undergirding this philosophy. A very brief set of theological axioms is provided here, summarizing the basic position of the theological statements in Appendix A.

1. God at work in the world. Though the questions of faith are never easy and the pattern of divine activity is often unclear, we confess that God is working purposefully in history and will prevail.

2. Jesus Christ and the new world of the converted. We accept Jesus Christ as the Supreme Revelation of God. In His name people are called to join the new order of God, to accept God s judgments and priorities instead of society's, to live as new people. Faith in Christ reconciles the person to God and to his neighbor and gives him freedom from rebellion and perverted values. He is free to enjoy God's good creation and participate in the new life God intends for His people.

3. The "pioneering minority" church. We assume that the community of faith is more than an established church; rather it is continually being formed and reformed through the work of the Spirit of God. The people of God are not confined to any one race or clan or nation. Rather they are called from loyalty to the natural order to a new loyalty in response to the call of God through Jesus Christ.

4. The new community of the converted: its mutual responsibilities. Within the brotherhood members are expected to support each other in service and mutual discipline.

5. The new community of the converted: its life in the world. Members of the Christian church are called to a life of suffering love. We cannot expect the unconverted to submit to this as a law, but it is both a possibility and expectation for those who are willing to join God's people.

6. The Bible and the church. The Bible is the criterion by which the faithfulness of God's people is measured. The church receives the Bible as the source of its own history, as the Word of God and the authoritative guide to faith in Christ and the life of discipleship. Church education needs to be informed by and give proper emphasis to the teaching of the Bible.

7. Personal responsibility to choose. Though we recognize that each person is influenced by his background and environment, we affirm his responsibility to decide which of the many peoples in the contemporary world he wants to call his own and which way his life shall count. Church education is concerned about the will as well as the mind.

Though lacking the range of thought found in the theological statements, these seven ideas speak briefly for the statements and undergird the philosophical principles which follow.

3

Mennonite Philosophy of Education:

Basic Questions

The general failure to educate is not the result of the lack of goodwill, but rather the result of the immense complexities and difficulties involved in the educational experience — *Andrew M. Greeley*

As noted above, the person who teaches must give some thought to his reasons. This study, however, has led us to begin farther back than the work of the individual teacher or institution. We are concerned with the comprehensive issues touching the very existence of education. The work of an institution or individual becomes meaningful only as an expression of this larger whole.

In this basic philosophy section, the issues will be posed as questions. The questions are general and could be discussed in the context of general education. Our concern, however, is with education as practiced by the church.

What are the important questions a philosophy of education must face? We have found two especially as implied by our title: the question of *purposes* and the question of *process*. In addition we believe *educational settings and learning relationships* are important, and our assignment has called for us to consider questions of learning and *learning theories*. And although we have used our own theological assumptions as a beginning point rather than any of the classic or current *philosophies of education*, we will have some observations about the relative validity of these philosophies from our standpoint as church

17

educators. These concepts will form the outline of the discussion which follows.

Question 1: What Are the Purposes of Education?

Education is not for itself alone. It needs to be related to a greater cause.

1. The purposes of education are defined in the *context of the purposes of a people*. For example, national, state, or provincial education tends to support the goals of the sponsoring people. Broadly speaking, the goals of a politically organized people are political and economic security, civilization (being able to live together decently), and vision for the "good life" however conceived. Educational goals for this people will emphasize *identity* and loyalty, development of *skills* needed for an adequate supply of workers such as miners, barbers, social workers, and scientists, together with *additional emphases* which arise from its concept of civilization and the good life.

2. *The people of God* are a distinct people with a unique calling and a special set of educational goals. What are the purposes of the people of God? *Reconciliation* is the term used in our theological statements (Point II) to summarize this people's task: "The covenant people exist as a reconciled and reconciling community. . . . As the first fruits of the new humanity, the church is to be God's servant and witness to His purposes for all creation and for all mankind."

To become and remain a people, the people of God must educate to make their *history* and *identity* clear. As a people within a larger society, they also educate in part to *counteract the influence* of that society upon them. They educate also to *train themselves* to *serve* as God's reconciling people. Still another educational purpose is fulfilled when they *educate others* as a form of service and as an opportunity for Christian witness.

These specific educational goals will differ for different groups. In fact, at least four groups may merit educational attention from the church: (1) members; (2) children of members; (3) nonmember adults; (4) children of nonmembers. Purposes in providing education and the nature of the program will

18

vary from group to group. For example, young persons need to learn the history and purposes of the people of God and what is to be expected of them if they choose to join. "In education, the teacher and those he represents transmit a selection of the experiences and insights they have found valuable in their generation to the next. . . . They seek to make their successors independent in their own right — able to think for themselves, to express their thoughts and feelings, and to live in individual and collective response to God's initiative and leading."[5]

Adult members need training and retraining for their part in the people's mission of reconciliation. They need perspective to help them accept and understand life with its changing experiences and opportunities. Persons not affiliated with the church may be educated as service to them and instruction in what it would mean for them to join the people of God.

3. For an educational process to have integrity, the *values taught to the young must be practiced by the adults.* This is true for any people, but especially the people of God whose values run counter to those of a prevailing culture. This responsibility for concrete expression of values is borne by persons individually and by the group as a whole in the institutions organized and supported by the people.

Social scientists generally view with skepticism the effectiveness of formal education in teaching values. The family, the neighborhood, peer group, and employment are considered to have more influence on values than formal schooling.[6]

4. *The educational program also needs continued scrutiny* to guard against professional self-serving and related pressures which may cause it to lose touch with the identity and needs of the sponsoring people. Educational institutions and programs need to be specifically tailored to relate to the objectives of the people for whom the institution has been organized.[7]

An educational program left to itself tends to go in a circle. It needs a larger cause. An example of education related to a larger cause is John Fischer's hypothetical "Survival University," whose concern would be human ecology, whose motto would be "What must we do to be saved?" and in which every course would in some way help to answer that question. The University of Wisconsin at Green Bay is already operating on this type of plan.[8]

This is not to suggest that church schools must go into ecology, but to emphasize the need for valid goals, chosen with Christian perspective. The church will be expected to undertake such renewal and reformulation under the guidance of the Spirit and in the light of the Scriptures.

In summary, church education is concerned to teach the meaning of Christian peoplehood. It should not only describe but also demonstrate the love for God and man which is the traditional manner of the people of God. Its goal is a person who will be informed about his heritage and articulate about his faith. He will see himself as a person of value and respect himself and others. He will be ready to contribute his efforts toward the service of mankind and the development of Christian brotherhood.

Question 2: What Are the Elements of the Educational Process?

What then do we do in education?

1. A basic component of all education is *background information and perspective* on the stream of people of which the learners are a part. Whether he is studying to be an American, a Christian, or a violin maker, he needs some history of the background and customs of his people. What a person finally becomes is conditioned by his choice of a tradition — his own or some alien background. Nobody can start in any other way. Jesus, the most original of persons, began His career with a thorough saturation in His own tradition. "Even when a person opposes these traditions in order to overcome this or that prejudice or form that has become empty, he still lives with the tradition. By criticizing what has been transmitted, a man swings himself to a new level. But he still pushes off from what has been transmitted in order to make the leap beyond it."[9]

Education, however, is not concerned to simply transmit a tradition. The process of education should result in the continuing restatement, redefinition, and reformulation of the peo-

20

ple's uniqueness and calling. For the people of God, this renewal is a response to the challenge of the changing environment and new perspective received from the Scriptures. Evaluation and innovation should be expected. This pattern of openness allows for adjustment to changes as a result of new insights by the educating group as well as those imposed by events beyond control of the educators.

2. *A second component* of education is the *teaching of values*, the distilled experience of what the people have considered important. A more comprehensive definition of value from Clyde Kluckhohn is as follows: "A value is a conception . . . of the desirable which influences the selection from available modes, means, and ends of action."[10]

In other words, values dictate choices and priorities and will thus vary from group to group. Section III of the Theological Statements in Appendix A suggests the stance of the disciple with regard to certain commonly accepted values. The church in its teaching program will need to articulate its own distinctive values, particularly its emphasis on loyalty to Christ and His Word first of all.

3. *Training in the skills* needed to function in the society of which the learner is a part is a *third important element* in education. What does he need to be able to do to take his place as a responsible member of the group? For an auto mechanic, this means ability to service and repair an auto engine. For the scientist it calls, among other things, for understanding of certain techniques in his field. For the researcher it requires ability to use the library card catalog.

The Christian needs to learn specific skills needed to serve and to witness with his brothers in the name of Christ. In fact, discipleship might be viewed as a skill: a way of functioning as a follower of Christ toward the fulfilling of Christian purposes. As such it needs to be described and demonstrated so the person may understand it, accept or reject it as a way of life, and learn the details of how to practice it.

4. *Structuring a personal view of reality* is, from the learner's standpoint, probably the most important part of educa-

tion. He uses background information and perspective, his own values and the skills he has learned, to answer the following questions: Who am I? What is real? To what shall I commit myself? The young person's education and growing-up process is largely concerned with finding satisfactory answers to these questions.

Post-Freudian psychologists refer to "modeling" as the process whereby the young person unconsciously selects from others the character traits he will accept. In a broader concept, Marc Belth speaks of model building in which the learner puts together his own model of reality under the guidance of the teacher. Three sources of models he mentions are history, current experience, and imagination. But all three, he says, are interrelated.[11] For the Christian student, the Bible and church history are important sources of models.

The most obvious source of personal models is found in the persons with whom the learner has significant experience. One would generally expect these to be parents and teachers, but other models may on occasion be more effective. Factual learning becomes really meaningful only in the context of personal relationships. For the Christian church, Jesus Christ is the chief model and authority figure. The ultimate educational mission of the church is to lead persons to accept and commit themselves to Him. "Identification with Christ," says Stinnette, "is both the means whereby idolatry is broken and the end goal of our quest for identity."[12]

At the same time, the educational process should assist the learner in constructing a view of reality which is really his own. By helping him clarify his values and begin to function on the basis of them, the educator aids the young person to come to terms with himself, his parents and his tradition and so decide what manner of person he will be.

As change and innovation are crucial for the educational program and institution, so the young learner needs to experience the reality of Christian discipleship rather than just being told about it. Each new generation inherits a set of customs and institutions which were new and somewhat radical to the fathers, but which appear old and stale to the sons if not meaningfully presented and dynamically experienced. Jacob Loewen has observed that Mao Tse-tung's Red Guard organization appeared to be an attempt to give the young a revolutionary experience so they might have the same understanding of revolution as the old group. He wonders if the same pattern can be adopted by the Christian church. In other words, can each generation in some sense become "first generation Christians"?[13]

History, values, skills, and *view of reality:* are these all that an educational program has to offer the learner? Others would state it differently. Andrew M. Greeley adds *developing critical intelligence* and *the training of scholars* as basic goals of education.[14] These are acknowledged here as important goals. The former would seem to be included in *structuring a personal view of reality* and the latter appears to be included in *skills* and particularly related to graduate education. Seminary education is the only graduate education sponsored by the Mennonite Church for which this philosophy is developed. Thus this purpose may receive less emphasis in a philosophy statement intended for the total church.

Question 3: What Relationships and Social Settings Will Foster Learning?

1. *Education in the history and values of the Christian tradition and in the skills* required to serve in it are best accomplished in an *experience of community.* Community as used here does not refer to a geographical unit or to the church generally as the Christian community. Rather it designates a size of group and physical proximity which permit first-name acquaintance and primary relationships.

As important as the facts to be learned is the opportunity of knowing the teacher and fellow learners. There is accumulating research evidence that 300 to 350 is the optimum size peer group to which a college student can relate meaningfully. Regardless of the dedication of the persons involved, the physical and psychological limitations inhibit community in larger groups. This suggests that a college larger than this should be organized in modules of 300 to 400 persons.[15]

Though the research referred to did not include study of the most ideal size for a church congregation, it is common knowledge that these may easily become too large for community. It is probable that the same and possibly much smaller limits would apply. The dynamics of congregational size and relationships need consideration on a separate basis from those of a residential college.

2. *Why this strong emphasis on community?* As noted above, there is the *opportunity for personal interaction* with teachers and other learners. If it be accepted that truth is personal and personally transmitted, it becomes clear that personal acquaintance is crucial for an effective educational program.

Experience in community provides opportunity to *articulate and test developing ideas* in an atmosphere of trust and acceptance. Mutual support and correction enable the learner to begin to know himself and to see the nature of his potential contribution to the group and society.

The experience of community also provides an appropriate setting for *governance and control.* A disciplined Christian community exercises control, but in a redemptive rather than vindictive spirit. Standards are interpreted for the benefit of all and not for the convenience of one or a few persons. Governance in the mass, in a situation in which individual members do not talk about what they have in common and in which indeed there may be little interaction of any kind does not hold the possibilities that are available in governance in human-scale units characterized by genuine community.

3. *The family is the initial community* of learning. In the family the child learns basic *communication skills* and *methods of relating* to other persons. His concept of *sexuality* and understanding of male and female *roles* is based on experience in the family. *Socialization* and development of *conscience* begin here. Here is laid the foundation for *values* and *priorities.* The child who learns a sense of self-worth in the family will take this with him wherever he goes.

Today, however, the influence of the family has been replaced for many children by other primary groups. Since the developing person must learn his basic skills and values from someone, this basic education is received from whichever source has the most influence on him. The educational program of a voluntary group such as the church will need to take into account the individual's varied and possibly dysfunctional prior and current learnings.

Question 4: What Theory of Learning Shall We Prefer?

The development of our philosophical understandings in the areas of learning theory and personality theory are conditioned by the following factors.

We begin with our basic concept of the nature of man as a choosing and decision-making agent in a social matrix. We interpret the changing views of man's nature in the light of the biblical position that man is sinful. Man is assumed to be free enough to be held responsible, yet the nature and extent of his choices are limited by the environment in which he finds himself, and by failure of will.

We take seriously also the experimental findings and theoretical models which are part of our intellectual heritage in the field of psychology. At present there is no one theory of personality or learning that is completely satisfactory from the viewpoint of Christian education. However, the various themes serve as useful checks and balances on each other and as sources of hypotheses for testing.

Each of the theories listed below tends to claim a degree of wholeness which if granted would make it an idol to which all other values must be sacrificed. Our prior commitment as people of God and our broader concern for learning as a social phenomenon will deliver us from complete devotion to any one of them. They will be affirmed for all they can contribute to the service of man, but will be challenged at the point where they threaten to become autonomous, and will be systematically rejected at the point where they begin to enslave man.

Following are examples of some potentially useful theories with certain of their implications.

1. *Freudian and post-Freudian theories.* Useful elements

25

from these theories are the emphasis on the unconscious, the importance of early childhood experiences, and the assumption that the person goes through a series of distinct phases in his maturation process, with each phase preparing the person for a certain kind of learning. Thus to attempt to impose a certain learning too soon or withhold it too long may do violence to the learner.

This kind of thinking correlates with the Anabaptist concern for responsible maturity in deciding to follow Christ. The traditional Mennonite concept of the "age of accountability" has something in common with Erik Erikson's theory of the adolescent search for identity. Following this thinking, one should not expect a full discipleship commitment before a person has come to his "identity crisis."

Erikson has provided an additional dimension which is of interest to church educators: An emphasis on the psychosocial nature of the person's development. He holds that "man's psychosocial survival is safeguarded only by vital virtues which develop in the interplay of successive and overlapping generations, living together in organized settings."[16] In other words, the development of the human personality is a complex process involving significant interpersonal relations as well as the unfolding of a biological organism.

2. *Behaviorism* is of interest to church education because of its insistence on clear-cut, testable goals, and the importance of doing as an expression of being. An educational effort has been effective only when it has produced the outcomes it is meant to produce in the form of changed behavior in the learner. Behaviorism also alerts us to the fruitfulness of positive rather than negative incentives in teaching, and stresses the important fact that experience conditions people.

Behaviorism calls on the church to specify the kinds of behaviors it wishes to develop. It then offers to describe the kinds of experiences which will lead people in the direction of these desirable behaviors.[17]

3. From a Christian standpoint it would appear that both Freudian and behaviorist theories tend at times to emphasize the influence of environment at the expense of individual oppor-

tunity and responsibility. It is thus of interest to note that in contrast to these two theories is the *personalist* psychology of Gordon Allport, whose theory stresses the self-containment of personality, motivation as a factor of present experience (not merely earlier pressure), and self-consciousness. A somewhat similar point of view is the logotherapy of Viktor E. Frankl, who holds that "man is *not* fully conditioned and determined; he determines himself whether he will give in to conditions or stand up to them."[18] Also worthy of attention is the work of cognitive psychologists such as Jean Piaget and Jerome Bruner.[19]

These theories are potentially useful to church educators as examples for educational strategy and criteria to measure effectiveness. Others could be mentioned, but these illustrate the point to be made. To the extent that these theories are available to serve man rather than the disciplines themselves, we can use them in a Christian approach to learning.

An alternate and much more ambitious approach would be to attempt to articulate a Christian theory of learning. Robert R. Boehlke attempted such a specifically Christian theory which he labeled "Creation Engagement." "Creation" in his theory refers to God's work in Christian education. "Engagement" refers to the learner's part. According to Boehlke, since it "includes such meanings as interaction, encounter, commitment, and mutually accepted responsibilities, it is able to integrate the essential insights of learning theory." Boehlke's effort is commendable, but the semantic difficulties involved with this subject suggest that it needs more thorough evaluation through research and experimentation.[20]

Christian learning cannot be conceptual or environmental only, nor habit alone, nor for the individual alone. No theory of learning can be satisfactory for the church which fails to recognize that Christian learning has many dimensions and that man is called of God to make decisions which affect his destiny.

Question 5: How Shall We Regard the Classic and Current Philosophies of Education?

It was stated above that we have used our "Theological

Statements" as a basis on which to develop a practical philosophy of education. We have thus not selected any one of the extant philosophies as a source for justifying our position on reality, truth, and value.

However, it may be proper for us to state an opinion about the current philosophies as viewed from our point of view. The following evaluations are based on Lester Brubaker's work.[21]

Five philosophies are described in the report: Idealism, Realism, Neo-Thomism, Pragmatism, and Existentialism. Each views God, man, and the universe from a different point of view. In a summary section on strengths and weaknesses of each position, he groups Neo-Thomism with Realism and thus includes four summaries of strengths and weaknesses.

Idealism is found strong in its emphasis on the nonmaterial and the value of persons along with its concern for meaning rather than rote learning. On the other hand Idealism tends to hold in higher regard people with high reasoning ability; it also tends toward a low view of the body and material things combined with an optimism about man that often does not square with the facts.

Realism and *Neo-Thomism* properly emphasize order and stability in the world. They hold that sense perception as well as conception is important and have a strong feeling for moral order. Conversely they are weak in reducing the freedom of man. They tend to make him a puppet and to overemphasize material and scientific values.

Pragmatism is strong on emphasizing action and involvement of the learner, weak because it denies a place for God. Man is seen as merely a part of nature and there are no objective standards.

Existentialism properly calls attention to the importance of the individual and the need for personal commitment. It emphasizes relationships as more important than knowledge only. But from our point of view this philosophy errs in making each person his own authority and in overemphasizing the present at the expense of the past and the future.

The careful reader will note from this brief summary that

aspects of all four of these philosophies are present in our own philosophy outlined above. They are part of our intellectual heritage and we may use them in the same manner that we make use of theories of personality and learning.

In line with *Idealism* we believe in the value of persons and in the need for each to come to terms with the meaning of his experience.

In line with *Realism* we believe there is recognizable order in the world and that history has meaning.

Along with *Pragmatism* we believe that learning is related to the life of a whole people. It is not confined to schools alone.

We are impressed, as is *Existentialism,* with the importance of choice.

In summary our philosophy holds the following as important:

1. The people of God are a distinct people with a distinct calling and unique educational goals. They must educate to
   a. transmit their history and make their identity clear;
   b. train in the skills needed to carry on the work they consider important;
   c. teach the values they consider important;
   d. help the young develop his own personal view of reality.

2. The task of education is carried on not only in schools, but it is the work of the whole people. In fact, it is only as they are practiced by the group that values taught in schools can be expected to be taken seriously.

3. The educational task is seen as a part of the people's faithfulness to God and thus should be subjected to regular scrutiny to keep it in touch with the goals and needs of the people of God.

4. The ultimate purpose of education as practiced by the people of God is to aid in living as a reconciled and reconciling people.

.4

Mennonite Educational Strategy:
A Proposed Ten-Point Formula

*Live life, then, with a due sense of responsibility, not as men
who do not know the meaning and purpose of life, but as
those who do. — Ephesians 5:15.*°

What kind of educational strategy is needed for the philosophy of
education described above? Because the church is seen as a people
within a people, who are called both to be separate from and
servants to the larger people, its educational program should be
concerned to equip Christians to function in this role. They should
learn the facts of the human situation, come to understand the
limitations of human effort, be made familiar with the biblical
world view and with Christian values. They need to learn the
skills required for ministry in the work of witness and reconciliation.

Thus whatever educational institutions are formed or re-
tained should be operated as an expression of Mennonite vocation
and mission. As a minority group, Mennonites need not expect
to participate or train for participation in everything in the
larger society. Nor need they be concerned to provide all services necessary for their own life in society. Their relations with
culture should be flexible and tentative to allow for innovation
and adaptation to changing circumstances. More specifically

°From *The New Testament in Modern English,* © J. B. Phillips. 1958. Used
by permission of The Macmillan Company.

the following ten points of strategy appear to grow out of the philosophy discussed in the preceding chapter.

1. *The congregation as a decision-making and educating agency is the basic institution in Mennonite educational strategy.*

A congregation is ideally a very flexible and versatile entity. The congregation serves as a visible representation of the people of God. It can function without its own building or professional clergy and thus may be constituted anywhere there are enough like-minded people to call for its organization. On the other hand it is in a position to support and draw on the services of professional leaders or other institutions to enrich its discerning and educating functions.

The congregation is the logical community to invite persons to commit themselves to Christ and the life of Christian discipleship. It is in a position to serve persons of all ages and conditions, all four groups mentioned earlier as within the church's educational field: (1) members; (2) children of members; (3) nonmembers; (4) children of nonmembers.

Thus the congregation is the logical agency to provide family life education and other types of adult education needed to undergird its program. It provides the context for moral and religious education of the young while still based in the family. The congregation should also serve alone or in cooperation with others as a sponsoring agency for institutions needed to respond to educational problems in a specific situation.

In fact, education for family life and educational services to families are two fruitful strategies which have not received the attention they deserve. As noted previously, the family is the basic unit shaping the child's personality and teaching him values. Every effort should be made to educate parents so the family may be strengthened rather than simply attempting to make up for the failures of the family through corrective education in other institutions.

This would attempt to meet the persons' emotional needs and to teach them how to function in their homes and in society

31

so that they may serve as well as be served. Paul Tournier holds that a child who learns a sense of personal worth and security in his family can be at home anywhere in the world. The one without these may spend his whole lifetime in searching for them.[22]

2. Changing circumstances and a variety of situations call for variation in educational organization.

It need not be expected that the educational purposes of the people of God will be accomplished in a uniform manner. If there is provision for a discerning congregation, the nurture of family life, teaching of Christian values, and the effective influence of significant teachers on the learner, the educational patterns may vary according to preference and circumstance. The Baptist churches in Russia carry on with no educational institutions except the congregation and the home. This may not be the most desirable pattern, but at least it is notable that they survive and grow.

Paul M. Lederach observes that "The people of God are formed as they respond to God in repentance and faith, to what He has done in Jesus Christ, and allow the Holy Spirit to work in and through them in the world. Becoming in a specific time and place requires that those engaged in the teaching ministry, for example, hear and answer the Word of God instead of continuing without question the many, many good teaching agencies that have been borrowed or have come upon us."[23]

The question of how much of the educational program a church must control to be effective requires careful discernment. Whatever educational strategy is devised should be done in the context of the needs and opportunities for education in the larger culture. As stated above, Mennonites need not attempt to participate in all that is done by the larger society, nor on the other hand need they provide all of their own services.

The following would seem to be legitimate reasons for the church to engage in institutionalized educational efforts: (1) the need to train her own people for their vocation as Christians; (2)

the opportunity to provide models of how education really ought to be done; (3) a context for the growth of personhood through an integration of knowledge and values in a Christian environment.

Not enough research has yet been done to prove that one institutional pattern or age-level school is more effective than another in the teaching of values. A churchwide survey of Mennonite young people discovered "few if any significant differences" between those attending church-sponsored high schools and those enrolled in state schools. In reporting these data, however, Paul M. Lederach observes that "this does not mean that the value of the church-related high school is undercut. . . . To discern the worth of the Mennonite high school to the ongoing life of the church now and in the days ahead requires more than an analysis of the items of this research."[24]

Similarly Andrew Greeley and Peter Rossi concluded that Catholic religious education is cumulative in its influence on religious behavior and social attitudes. They observed, however, that in any attempt to set priorities, the level of schooling recommended for elimination is one in which a given speaker is not working. They also concluded that although Catholic schools have been effective and will likely continue, their presence is not essential for the preservation of the Catholic Church.[25]

The Mennonite Church has not responded in a uniform manner to the task of educating its young people. Statistics from the *Mennonite Yearbook* show that although there are other educational institutions, the Sunday school has the largest enrollment of Mennonite young people.

Fifteen church high schools are reported and 67 elementary schools with a total enrollment of 7,285. Mennonite Sunday schools report 45,705 pupils ages 6 to 17. Thus the enrollment in elementary and secondary schools is about 16 percent of the Sunday school enrollment.[26]

The statements which follow in this document are written with the present situation in mind. It is recognized that exact agreement on the best institutional strategy is not likely and that local conditions may differ sufficiently that a pattern which is valid in

33

one community would not be equally so in another.

The question of which level or levels of education and the specific role of each needs further study among Mennonites. (The question of the relative danger of cholesterol in the diet of Americans is also a hard question. It is receiving more research attention!) While we wait for further work in this direction, the following observations are proposed concerning the use of present educational patterns.

3. *There is need for formal church programs on at least some levels for education of children and young people.*

More than the Sunday school is needed. Today the training of the young is more and more professionalized. For example, there is physical education in schools and many children receive private music lessons. Home economics is an accepted part of elementary and secondary education. Thus it is expecting too much for the informal influence of the home and the work of unpaid volunteers to carry the full weight of instruction in the Bible and the heritage and values of the church and their relevance to the fields of knowledge and experience. This is not meant to overlook the positive contribution of many excellent Sunday school teachers. It is simply saying that they lack the time and structures for accomplishing what is needed.

One form of response to this problem is the establishing of church-sponsored elementary and secondary schools. These provide the advantages of freedom to innovate, generally small size, control of curricula, and approved role models. In some local situations a church-sponsored elementary or secondary school can provide the total education of the child.

Another model of professional education is a program of released time, after school, Saturday or Sunday education, which could be correlated with nonprofessional programs such as the Sunday school. Such a program is concerned to see that the young person gets a basic acquaintance with the Bible, church history, and Christian values. Of particular importance is the interpretation of his other educational and informal experiences in the light of Christian faith. No small part of the educational function is the opportunity for the young to be exposed to teachers who represent Christian values.

The importance of religious education was supported recently by Joan Ganz Cooney, originator of the children's television program, *Sesame Street*. "If I had only one hour for religious teaching, I would teach history. . . . The best one can do is to teach about Jesus Christ — who He was historically, what He taught, and what He believed. Get them to discuss Him. . . .

"At seven they love to discuss. I went to a Catholic school and I remember just arguing and arguing with the priest. . . . This played a large role in who I am and how I function. . . . Then there was a high school teacher whose class met no more than twice a week. He talked about poverty long before it was fashionable. He played a decisive role with most of us."[27]

On the youth level, spiritual retreats along with counseling and activity programs might well be included or take the place of the structured program for younger children. A number of Mennonite district conferences have begun to provide professional youth leaders on at least a part-time basis.

Furthermore, the facilities needed for such programs could be used for related activities to supplement the inadequacies of education generally. Examples would be remedial reading or study help to aid the weaker student in keeping up with others. Such a program would be an authentic expression of the church's concern for people and an opportunity for Christian witness.

One Mennonite school reports the following strategy as a way of serving a variety of persons: (1) a modest tuition charge with the balance of the educational cost provided by the sponsoring church; and (2) remedial help for slow learners to keep them in the same classes as fast learners.

In fact, Mennonite educational efforts would do well to go farther in deliberately seeking out the underprivileged and children of minority groups. This kind of deliberate focus toward those in need of service should help to keep a program or school from catering only to upper- and middle-class patrons who

35

are well able to pay for it.

4. *The Mennonite idea of brotherhood calls for the education of everyone for a ministry rather than only the training of leaders.*

The mission of the church as described in the Theological Statements (Point IV) calls for the participation of all members in its life and ministry. However, it is not necessary or desirable that every person should have the same educational program.

It should not be expected, for example, that all Mennonites must go to college or that Mennonite colleges should serve all possible types of educational needs. In fact, Voluntary Service administrators report that although college-trained people have some skills that the non-trained lack, they sometimes can be less effective than those without this training. The college people are usually better at conceptualizing and organizing programs. These are necessary skills for an effective VS program, but persons with such skills sometimes prefer to work in formal settings rather than to relate informally to people in need. College-trained social workers tend, for example, to prefer working in a formal program under a qualified director. Thus sometimes the untrained are more flexible in placement and more willing to work informally with people and this can be more effective.

An overall educational strategy will recognize that programs such as Voluntary Service have educational as well as service significance. There would thus be a place for more cooperation between educational institutions and service boards in the orientation and debriefing of service workers.

It is assumed, however, that all members need a basic orientation in the history and understanding of our faith. One might expect this to come from the congregation, particularly if the professional program described in Item 3 above is taken seriously.

However, additional special programs will be needed. An example of this has been the Summer Seminar for Graduate Students, an attempt to provide a concentrated orientation to biblical and Mennonite history and thought. Other less advanced programs might appeal to high school graduates who do not go to college.

A model that should be tested more widely is the one outlined by Albert J. Meyer in his "Study of Church-Related Academic Sub-communities or Other Academic Resources on University Campuses." This is a modified form of church-sponsored college education in which there is opportunity for an intense experience of community and the teaching of Christian values through Christian faculty leaders. At the same time the student has access to the curricular variety of a university, which goes beyond the possibilities of the church college. This pattern, say Pattillo and MacKenzie, "helps to bridge the gap between religiously oriented and secular education. It fits the realities of a religiously pluralistic society."[28]

An educational strategy should also take into account the individual's need for lifelong learning. The responsibility to educate has not ceased once the person has graduated from the church's formal program. New experiences and opportunities call for new learning in order to fulfill the personal and group ministry.

Whatever its failings, this is one value of adult education in the Sunday school. Much of it has too narrow a base, and there is lack of urgency on the part of both learner and teacher. But it contains the possibilities for innovation and learning if both groups are prepared to take it seriously.

Several facts of life today call attention to the increasing importance of adult education. For one, the increase in life-span adds to the length of time one is known as "adult." In addition, the potential for change is such that a person may change location and/or employment a number of times during his life. Both are potential threats to his person, but may also be an opportunity for learning.

In fact, occupational education may be forced upon him. At the same time, the church has the opportunity to provide education for meaning. "There is an awakening of concern for adults among Christian educators," says Arnold Cressman. "Therefore, it is time to discover what can be most helpful to them. We must not just extend to the adult level what we have been doing for children. . . .

"Adults . . . are capable of taking the raw material of biblical principles and manufacturing new practical answers to questions which have never been asked before."[29]

5. *Educational programs should reflect the church's objectives.*

Not only should the church be clear about its reasons for certain church educational programs. Having satisfied itself that these are needed, the next step is to fashion a curriculum which gives evidence of concern for the goals which called it into being.

A first concern is for teachers who will be satisfactory role models. Beyond this is the basic question of what distinctive emphases and methods are needed to provide education for Christian peoplehood. Should the Mennonite history student, for example, learn all about the world's wars? Or are there other facts which are of more importance to him?

There is no place for carelessness in curriculum design. Yet there are other criteria of effectiveness than those provided by state accrediting agencies. For example, John A. Hostetler found that children from Amish parochial schools compared favorably with control groups on a series of standardized tests.[30] If the Amish educational system prepared students adequately in this respect, it seems likely that the program was otherwise satisfactory from the Amish standpoint. These results would encourage church educators to take the liberty necessary to devise an educational program suited to their own purposes.

6. *There is need for coordination of educational programs among agencies concerned about the same goals.*

A Sunday school and a church-sponsored elementary or secondary school serving the same children should not provide programs which overlap. Rather they should coordinate programs so they may complement each other.

The same is true of the relationship between education on various levels. It would seem there should be a means of evaluation developed to discern the level of religious understanding among college applicants, for example. This could provide stimulation and guidance to high school and congregational Bible and church history teaching. In addition it would give college religion teachers an idea of the level of religious instruction for which the student is ready. Might it not also remind the student that there are other important fields of knowledge beyond those evaluated in the usual standarized tests?

Coordination is also important to make best use of the influence and resources of an educational institution beyond its specific direct function to students on its campus. The faculty of a formally organized educational institution is a resource for activity and leadership for congregations adjacent to the institution and to denomination-wide agencies. Discovering how this may come about calls for openness from both the institution and the leadership of adjacent congregations.

7. *Personal relationships should be emphasized in education more than buildings.*

Mennonite congregational leaders' speak casually of building costs in terms of hundreds of thousands while college administrators now think in the millions. This is a symbol of the extent of the church institutional building boom in which Mennonites have been involved since World War II.

The implications of our philosophy would de-emphasize expensive buildings. Rather, Mennonite educational institutions on all levels should make quality of relationships at first priority. It is a time to stress making better use of existing facilities rather than the addition of building to building. Education is moving increasingly from the classroom into the "field." And the heirs of the radical Anabaptist vision do well to avoid the building of temples or monuments whether for First Mennonite Church or on a college campus.

In fact, some congregations might negotiate for the rent of

public buildings or conversely, church buildings which are empty most of the week could be made available for other uses. This would emphasize the Mennonite belief that the church is the people and that one building is no more "holy" than another.

Solid buildings give persons a sense of security and permanence. It may be easier to arouse enthusiasm for these than for teachers' salaries or enriched program. But monuments do not teach what we wish to convey.

8. *We should ask again what we are aiming to accomplish in Mennonite colleges.*

Earlier in the document preference is stated for emphasis on the Mennonite congregation as the basic educational unit. Beyond this it is suggested that educational institutions come and go. The precise organizational pattern should be a response to the needs of the times and the pressures of the environment in the light of the church's educational purposes. Innovation and experimentation are encouraged.

But what specifically does this mean for educational institutions currently sponsored by the church? One of the concerns calling for the present study was a lack of support for Mennonite higher education. The problem continues. In a time of affluence, it seems strange that there should be lack of money for education, but this is the way it is.

If one observes the path of church-related education, there appears a tendency for schools to move gradually from church support to support by other groups and eventually to lose ties with the church. For example, Harvard and Yale were originally church-related colleges. The question arises then whether there is an inevitable movement of the church-related college from sacred to secular. If so, has it then been a mistake and should it be abandoned? The time is here for Mennonite colleges and the Mennonite Church to take a fresh look at what they have in common and how they may serve each other in an effort to express the biblical faith rather than to emulate their secular counterparts.

A group of Mennonite mission administrators[31] saw the following advantages of education in a Mennonite secondary or higher educational institution: (1) it provides a broader acquaintance with the Mennonite Church; (2) it makes the student more articulate about Christian discipleship and Mennonite history; (3) there are more satisfactory role models in the persons of teachers and counselors whom the learner can trust; (4) the learner is helped to see the world from a Christian point of view. No school they know does this adequately, but graduates of Mennonite schools. as they have observed them, make better Mennonite missionaries than those who have not had this experience.

William T. Synder of Mennonite Central Committee remarked that the present MCC program would be impossible without Mennonite colleges. Indeed it is impossible to imagine the North American Mennonite Church without the influence of its colleges. Thinking Mennonites recognize their value.

It would be proper for Mennonite colleges to reaffirm their intention to be Mennonite Church-related. This would include communicating with the church constituency in order to understand and be understood. It would also include fashioning curricula in light of the objectives of the Mennonite Church and acquainting students with church leaders as people of significance. This is not to suggest that colleges and teachers must take their cues exclusively from the church, but rather that the church should be taken seriously, and vice versa.

Church schools are a way to orient students in the history and current activity of the church. More specifically they are in a position to train for responsible Christian churchmanship. It should be expected, for example, that graduates of Mennonite schools will be prepared to participate in the church's witness and service program regardless of their specialization and where they decide to live.

It seems clear, however, that Mennonite colleges, particularly, will need to structure experiences through which students will understand the need to choose between commitment and noncommitment to Christ. Young people from Mennonite communities vary in the degree of their commitment on entering college. The church will need to exist in real and visible form on the campus to the point where the student makes a clear choice as to whether he wishes to join the community of God's people on the campus or not. This Christian community on the campus may take a variety of forms. In whatever form, it cannot be abstract or invisible, but real, concrete, and visible so that students are given opportunities for genuine choice.

The care and discipline of a diverse group will be more feasible if the colleges are organized into small enough units for learners and teachers to know each other and be known in an intimate way. As noted on page 23 there is a limit to the size of group the college student can relate to effectively. Mennonite colleges need to be reorganized into smaller units in order to facilitate "community."

Mennonite colleges of the future may be of various kinds, located in various places and with a variety of structural relationships. Some of the colleges in the United States, for example, may engage in cooperative programs with neighboring institutions or with others more distant.

Whatever their format and location, the challenge to Mennonite colleges is to become "hotbeds" of Christianity. They should be expected to prepare graduates who are ready to affirm their Christian heritage, who care about people and their needs and who have the skills to serve these needs.

It is assumed Mennonite educational institutions will strive for excellence in teaching and will prepare students through training in abstract thinking and appropriate vocational skills. The accrediting associations are concerned about these matters. It is the thesis of this report that these may be accomplished while at the same time the program is deliberately altered as needed to train young persons for responsible Christian living.

9. *Seminary education is a special concern of the church.*

If Mennonite education through college age is done in a responsible church-related manner, is seminary education needed? If the colleges are expected to prepare graduates for churchmanship, what should a seminary do?

In the first place, as professional education is needed in order that children shall be properly instructed, so the church needs Bible scholars to help deliver us from alien mythologies. Many in the church are simply not prepared to confront the confusing winds of doctrine abroad today. Someone needs to carry on the scholarly work required to keep the Mennonite heritage in view.

In addition, it is worthwhile for some learners to explore the questions of faith on a graduate level. It is reported that not all seminary students today come for training in the work of the church; some are not clearly committed and wish to understand the Christian faith.

What about the traditional seminary function of training preachers? The first generation of seminary-trained Mennonite pastors is still at work, so it is too early for an objective evaluation of their influence on the church. The Ministerial Information Center maintained by the Executive Secretary of Mennonite General Conference recently found requests from churches for pastors outnumbering available persons by seven to one. A large majority of these churches were asking for men with seminary training.

The emphasis on professional work in society would suggest a place for the professionally trained minister, although his presence is a potential threat to the responsible churchmanship implied in this philosophy. The expectation of the churches suggests that if seminaries can train and commission pastoral leaders who are able to help the people in congregations discover and fulfill a mission, they will be seen as useful. D. Elton Trueblood suggests the use of the term "coach" as a designation for the spiritual leader in a congregation. He is concerned to discover and develop the abilities of others in the congregation in addition to serving along with them.[32] The implications of our philosophy would suggest that seminary education should be viewed objectively, the same as all other levels of church-sponsored education, and evaluated from the standpoint of whether it is helping to fulfill the ultimate goals of Mennonite education.

An important part of this evaluation will be the practice of the Anabaptist understanding that the scholar "had to be able to justify his position to the people, with Holy Spirit insight the people tested his interpretation."[33]

10. *There is need for evaluation to measure the results of Mennonite educational efforts.*

Though expensive, difficult, and sometimes tedious, evaluation is imperative as a way of checking on the assumptions and biases which educators bring to their work. The problems reported above from Greeley and Rossi show that evaluation should not be undertaken carelessly.

It should nevertheless be included in the program of Mennonite education. To have most value, such research should be done under the supervision of a general agency such as the Mennonite Board of Education. One possible method would be to formulate and field test a measure of Mennonite values and the adequacy of a person's view of reality.

This might be administered regularly to adults with a variety of Mennonite educational experiences at about the age of thirty. The intention would be for such a tool to aid in discovering which education route (if any) is more effective in teaching Christian discipleship.

In addition to this evaluation of educational "product," it is possible to evaluate the quality of the educational "process," using categories derived from this philosophy. The following set of rather general questions suggests the kinds of issues that should be raised in evaluating a specific Mennonite educational program.

(1) Are there outgroup as well as ingroup learners involved in the program?

(2) Are the education skills and knowledge provided adequate to accomplish the institution's goals?

(3) Does the institution facilitate or hinder the implementation of primary group values?

(4) Is there verifiable learning of Christian values?

(5) Is there recognition of both the church and the world in the environment and instruction?

(6) Is there a system for evaluation from the standpoint of the goals of the church?

(7) Is there opportunity for effective interaction with role models and among peers?

(8) Is the program able to lead people to Christ and the new birth?

(9) Is the institution able to lead persons to discipleship, and to provide for the ongoing education of the disciple?

(10) Does the education take into account the need for life-long learning and is there emphasis on the maturation of the whole person?

(11) Does the program encourage affective and attitudinal as well as cognitive learning?

(12) Does the educational process foster moral discernment and commitment?

(13) Does it foster compassion for others, concern for and capacity to change the world?

(14) Does the program prepare people to cope with the demands of life?

(15) Is the program sufficiently free from traditional standards to innovate as needed? On the other hand, are there corrective processes to safeguard the institution from its own autonomy or estrangement from the constituency's commitment and identity?

(16) Does the program create pilot models of what should be in the future?

(17) Is the institution concentrating its efforts on services which are not readily available otherwise?

(18) If it is a noncongregational agency, does it enhance the capacity for congregational brotherhood to "be the church"?

(19) Is there an authentic unity binding: (a) the *vision* of the institution used in winning support for it; (b) the priority *decisions* made in projecting program, staffing, and spending; (c) and the verifiable *learnings* of the "product"?

(20) Do the procedures of decision-making and governance have the character of brotherhood process, consensus, and renunciation of manipulation?

(21) Is the biblical world view available to the learner as a

distinct viable option?

(22) Does the learner find help in unmasking and criticizing the value assumptions he has unwittingly accepted in his earlier experience?

(23) If circumstances change, such as through depression or persecution, so as to destroy the institution, is there an alternate strategy? What would be the other good way to do the task if it were not done this way?

5

Education for Christian Maturity

The results of Mennonite educational efforts need to be measured, asserts the preceding section, in order to know to what extent they are reaching our goals.

In addition to the admitted difficulty of educational measurement, there is the added problem that church education involves the realm of the Spirit, who, said Jesus, is like the wind, working where He will without being tied to our expectations.[34] With this insight to keep us humble, we may attempt to describe some of the characteristics we hope might come from a serious response to an adequate Mennonite education. We may view this from both an individual and a community standpoint.

The goal of Mennonite education is a person who will be informed about his heritage and articulate about his faith. He will have a sense of identity and vocation as a Christian and will see his occupation as a way in which to serve Christ. He will see himself as a person of value and so will respect himself and others. He will possess emotional independence, the capacity for critical judgment, and willingness to be unpopular. He will be concerned about spiritual, social, and economic opportunity for the poor and the oppressed and will himself not become a slave of affluence. Loyalty to Christ and Christian values will deliver him from too great devotion to his home country. In fact he can be at home in any country, for as a Christian he is really a world citizen.

But the Christian is not only an individual; he is also a person in community. The ultimate goal of church education is Christian maturity and this is more properly designated as group than as individual maturity.

The characteristics of the type of church life our educational efforts should be helping to build need to be kept in focus. Devoted to Christ and respectful of its heritage, the group would be open to change and adjustment as needed to accomplish its task. Though open to and ready to learn from others, mature Christians are not readily swayed by public opinion, nor do they give their highest loyalties to short-term values.

Christian maturity is described best by Paul in Ephesians 4 where his vision was that "we all attain to the unity of the faith and of the knowledge of the Son of God, to mature manhood, to the measure of the stature of the fulness of Christ; so that we may no longer be children, tossed to and fro and carried about with every wind of doctrine. . . . Rather . . . we are to grow up in every way into him who is the head, into Christ."[35]

So be it.

Footnotes

1. Paton Yoder, "Toward a Mennonite Philosophy of Education Since 1890." A paper presented to the Philosphy of Christian Education Research Committee, September 13, 1968.

2. Paul Erb, "Long-Term Planning in Mennonite Education," *Gospel Herald*, 57:978, November 10, 1964.

3. Minutes of the Philosophy of Christian Education Study Committee, October 10, 1966, Item 8, p. 2.

4. Minutes of the Philosophy of Christian Education Research Committee, September 18, 1967, Item 6, p. 2.

5. Albert J. Meyer, "Needed: a Mennonite Philosophy of Higher Education," *Mennonite Life*, 17:3, January 1962.

6. Andrew Greeley and Peter Rossi, *The Education of Catholic Americans*, p. 7.

7. On the subtle danger of secular values invading a church college through the faculty see Calvin Redekop, "Education and Social Change Among Mennonites," a paper presented to the Philosphy of Christian Education Research Committee, Sept. 13, 1968, p. 29.

8. John Fischer, "Survival University: Prospectus for a Really Relevant University," *Harpers*, 239:14, September 1969. See also "Survival U. is alive and burgeoning in Green Bay, Wisconsin," *Harpers*, 242:20, February 1971.

9. Wolfhart Pannenberg, *What Is Man*, p. 126.

10. From Talcott Parsons and Edward A. Shils as reported by C. Ellis Nelson, *Where Faith Begins*, p. 49.

11. Marc Belth, *Education As a Discipline*, p. 291.

12. Charles R. Stinnette, Jr. *Learning in Theological Perspective*, p. 68.

13. Jacob Loewen, "Socialization and Conversion in the Ongoing Church,"

Practical Anthropology, 16:15, January-February, 1961.

14. William E. Brown and Andrew M. Greeley, *Can Catholic Schools Survive?* p. 8.

15. See Albert J. Meyer, "Study of Church-Related Academic Sub-communities or Other Academic Resources on University Campuses," pp. V-6 to V-8.

16. Erik H. Erikson, *Insight and Responsibility,* p. 114.

17. Paul S. Kurtz, "Personality Development and Learning Theory," a paper presented to the Philosophy of Christian Education Research Committee, September 13, 1968.

18. Viktor E. Frankl, *Man's Search for Meaning,* p. 206.

19. See Tom Alexander, "Psychologists Are Rediscovering the Mind," *Fortune,* 82:108 ff., November 1970.

20. Robert R. Boehlke, *Theories of Learning in Christian Education,* p. 187.

21. J. Lester Brubaker, "Current Philosophies of Education Developed and Evaluated from a Christian Perspective." A paper presented to the Philosophy of Christian Education Research Committee, September 13, 1968.

22. Paul Tournier, *A Place for You.* His basic point is developed in Chapters 1-3 and elaborated throughout the book.

23. Paul M. Lederach, *Reshaping the Teaching Ministry,* p. 69.

24. Paul M. Lederach, *Mennonite Youth,* p. 97.

25. Greeley and Rossi, *op. cit.* See especially pp. 7, 13, 14, 160, 181, 220.

26. *Mennonite Yearbook,* 62:16-21, 45, 1971.

27. Richard R. Gilbert, "Sesame Street," *Presbyterian Life,* 23, 24:34, December 15, 1970-January 1, 1971.

28. Manning M. Pattillo, Jr., and Donald M. MacKenzie, *Church-Sponsored Higher Education in the United States,* p. 182.

29. Arnold W. Cressman, "Christian Education in the Congregation." A paper presented to the Philosophy of Christian Education Education Research Committee, September 13, 1968.

30. John A. Hostetler, "Old Order Amish Child Rearing and Schooling Practices, a Summary Report," *Mennonite Quarterly Review,* 44:181-191, April 1970.

31. Paul N. Kraybill, Harold Stauffer, and Larry Newswanger, representing Eastern Mennonite Board of Missions and Charities, Salunga, Pa. Dorsa Mishler, Roy Yoder, James Kratz, and Wilbert Shenk of Mennonite Board of Missions and Charities, Elkhart, Ind., generally reinforced this opinion.

32. D. Elton Trueblood, *The Incendiary Fellowship,* pp. 43-54.

33. J. C. Wenger, "How Do We Discover the Meaning of the Biblical Message?" Unpublished paper read to the Mennonite Publication Board in March 1969, p. 14. See also John Howard Yoder, "The Hermeneutics of the Anabaptists," *Mennonite Quarterly Review,* 41:291-308, October 1967.

34. John 3:8.

35. Ephesians 4:13-15.

Appendix A

Theological Statements for Philosophy of Mennonite Education

The attached document is a specialized piece with a specific purpose. It was developed as background for philosophy of Mennonite education. The writers of the document are concerned that it should be understood and evaluated with this purpose in view.

It is not intended as a comprehensive confession of faith. Thus the materials and themes from the realm of theology were not selected with a view to balance or completeness as a doctrinal system. Instead it is an attempt to include topics which are capable of being given operational significance for thinking about education. If readers note the absence of important theological topics, we would wish to know what significance these topics have for the structuring of an educational process.

Because of this concern for functional relevance, the document in a number of places deliberately avoids the use of theological language. This does not mean that we reject theological concepts, but that we are trying to express relationships between God and man and between man and man in language which may meet on common ground the language of educational philosophy and principles.

Because of a concern for brevity, these statements omit significant reference to many important biblical themes and/or persons. The selection of Abraham as the representative father of the faithful, for instance, leaves aside certain other points which could be made more fully if Moses, David, and the prophets were also given extended attention. The interest in Abraham as a model grew in part out of the history of this research process and the persons involved in it. However, we believe it can also be justified on the grounds of similar references to Abraham in the New Testament.

The statements have been refined during two workshops arranged by the Philosophy of Christian Education Research Committee. They have been further refined by a mail consultation with a representative group of Mennonite theologians.

I. The nature of biblical faith

A. God is at work in history creating for Himself a people.
  1. The Bible deals with history and its meaning, not with detached philosophical speculation; with events and not timeless theory, with obedience and not disincarnate ideals. °

B. The creation of the covenant people is a work of the grace of God. It is done for this people, in spite of the people's inability to meet its own needs.
  1. Abraham is spoken of as the father of all believers because, like all persons of faith since him, he answered the call of God to become part of His people.
     a. Abraham forsakes security and lives toward the future.
     b. Abraham forsakes the unity of pagan society and civilization as given to him by the past and commits himself to a pilgrimage with God, not knowing exactly what is promised to him, but trusting God both for the certainty and goodness of the promise.
     c. Abraham is called out of the confusion of Babel, the fragmentation and conflict which human pride had brought down as judgment on a self-seeking society, and commits himself to becoming the father of a new community.
     d. Abraham accepts a new kind of life, in which he responds by faith to the promises and demands of the covenant. These demands are not opposed to his own welfare but are the means whereby God will bless him.
     e. The ultimate promise given Abraham is that through him the nations of the world shall be blessed.

C. God's creation of a covenant people is for the purpose of reconciling all things and all men with Himself. To this end Jesus Christ

---

° The Bible contains, and is also the source of, propositional truth of significance for man in every relationship.

is both the fulfillment of God's promise to Abraham and the initiator of a new covenant which is intended to include all mankind.

1. Jesus Christ is spoken of as the founder and perfecter of the faith because in His person the meaning of obedience to the call of God is realized.

   a. By His birth into the human condition.

   b. By His ministry to every dimension of the needs of men.

   c. By His death at the hands of rebellious men and for their sake to free them from the power and penalty of their rebellion.

   d. By His victory over death in the resurrection and ascent to the right hand of God.

   e. By His promised return to fulfill all God's purposes.

D. The same faith which sees God at work creating a people trusts Him to fulfill His purposes in the future.

   1. God is proclaimed to be in control of the course of history which will ultimately be brought to the fulfillment of the purposes He has set.

   2. God intervenes in the experience of societies and of individuals, altering the course of events for His purposes.

E. The same God who calls and creates the people is proclaimed the Creator of all things. (We understand creation in the new creation — Jesus Christ and the new community, a fulfillment of the Old Testament's testimony to the Creator.) Creation, then, as the work of God who is calling men into covenant, is seen as a purposive act of God's grace and goodness.

   1. When God created all things, He declared them good. All knowledge is first of all God's, all truth is His, all of man's activity is under His lordship.

   a. Man is given dominion or responsibility over nature. It is his responsibility to use it for God's purposes.

   b. Man is created male and female. Sexuality and the structure of the family into which man is born and within which he becomes himself are God's provision for the creation of personality.

   c. As Adam was first assigned the task of giving names to the animals, it is the function of man to discern meaning in the created world; to accumulate and interpret knowledge.

   d. The ordinary materials of life, food and drink, money, and social relationships, are the objects of the concern of God. There is no "secular" realm beyond the scope of His will.

2. Man's rebellion — which can also be spoken of as his subservience to Satan — has so distorted God's creation that it becomes his prison.

   a. Instead of exercising dominion over nature he makes it his idol.

   b. Sexuality and the family structure become perverted into sensuality and self-seeking indulgence.

   c. Knowledge is perverted into pride.

   d. Man attempts to put God in a compartment by the perverted use he makes of the distinction between the sacred and the secular, in order to maintain his rebellious freedom in the rest of his life.

   e. Sin is not merely a metaphysical entity but the historical reality of the rebellion of man; his limited capacity for good and bondage to evil, known theologically as "depravity."

II. The nature of the church and the meaning of membership

A. The covenant people exist as a reconciled and reconciling community and live in fellowship with God and with one another.

   1. To be a people is to have a common history. Israel looks back to how God had led Abraham and their fathers into Egypt, then through Exodus to Sinai and into the promised land. Christians look back to the life, death, resurrection, and ascension of Christ, to the gift of the Holy Spirit and to His continued working in their midst.

   2. Christians gather in testimony to the past action of God; their worship is commemoration and celebration of that past action.

   3. Christians gather with confidence in the continuing action of God. When the past faithfulness of God is commemorated and proclaimed, when Christians give and receive counsel, bind and loose, and renew their commitment to common obedience, then Christ is truly in their midst.

   4. Since the present and future action of God is in continuity with His action in the past, the Bible, which is the testimony to that past action, is the criterion for faithfulness of God's people in the present and the future. The church receives the Bible as the Word of God and the authoritative Guide to faith in Christ and the life of discipleship.

5. The church is not, as Israel was not, a "club" of individuals with similar interests who freely or arbitrarily gather together under their own initiative and power.

6. The church is not, as Israel was not originally called to be, a "nation" defending her identity like her pagan neighbors through the power of kingship after the Canaanite model.°

7. As the first fruits of the new humanity the church is to be God's servant and witness to His purposes for all creation and for all mankind. It is the society of the redeemed where His will is done through the renewing power of the Spirit and Word.

B. Membership is a matter of free adult decision.

1. Only "believers" (i.e., those who admit their need, renounce their past, and commit themselves to Christ and the church) are baptized. Persons are to be genuinely free to make this decision.

2. Infants are not baptized. The decision to be baptized requires awareness of the options, the sense of responsibility that goes with maturity, and a commitment to obedience to carry through the implications of that decision.

3. Religious liberty is assumed and social coercion is rejected. The church must be so structured that persons may freely enter on the basis of faith in Christ and commitment to discipleship. Those who reject these should be free to leave the church, though not without earnest warning.

4. Social freedom (from coercion) and psychological freedom (awareness of options) are not intrinsic to the human situation. They are enabled only by the grace of the call of God. Apart from this call, man is unfree, a slave of sin. The biblical/Anabaptist call for social and psychological freedom of choice must be distinguished from modern views of the innate moral freedom of man apart from God.

C. Membership is sharing within the life and fellowship of the congregation.

°"Israel" is here seen as a prefiguration of the church, which is only one of the meanings of the term. There are other perspectives from which Israel (ancient Israel or Judaism since Christ) can be viewed. These other views, however, do not have other implications for the meaning of membership in the church.

1. The Lord's Supper commemorates the work of Christ with the emblems of a common meal.
2. Members of the congregation commit themselves to the practice of mutual aid as each has need.
3. Members share in the exercise of the gift of ministry of each member for the upbuilding of the whole body.
4. Membership is total: every segment of life can be the subject of common interest and responsibility and a matter of common congregational concern.

D. Members of the congregation support one another with "binding and loosing"; with mutual admonition and forgiveness.
1. The congregation finds the will of God in common study and counsel with preaching, teaching, shepherding, and correction.
2. The congregation experiences and communicates reconciliation and forgiveness.
3. The congregation applies the guidance of Scripture, seeking and testing its meanings for the present, in conversation with the Christian brotherhood.
4. The congregation becomes the locus of the voice of the Holy Spirit for discerning God's will for the lives of the members.

E. Membership is participation in congregational mission.
1. All members are engaged in the mission of the congregation; there are not two classes of membership, mature missionary members and ordinary members.
2. Each member exercises his special gifts in the support and advance of congregational witness. (See Section IV for further explication of mission.)

III. The meaning of discipleship as relationship to Jesus Christ

A. The disciple turns away from other values to serve Christ.
1. This may include forsaking genuine values ("hating father and mother"), for the sake of a higher calling.
2. One must turn away from all unworthy values: from those which pride or sensuality or paganism would absolutize.
3. This calls for simplicity of life and vigilance in order to avoid becoming enslaved.
4. This may call for total rejection of certain pagan patterns, in which idolatry is discerned (graven images in the Old Testament, sacrifice to the image of Caesar in the New Testament).
5. In other cases the believer may rescue cultural values from idolatry and be enabled to use them without becoming their

slave (the New Testament's acceptance of eating meat offered to idols, the Old Testament pattern of temple music).

B. The disciple obeys Jesus Christ as master.
1. For Christ to be Lord means that He receives the disciple's exclusive loyalty: all other value must be defined in terms of relationship to Him.
2. Every dimension of life belongs within this obedience: there is no realm which is ruled by other standards.
3. For Christ to be Lord means that the disciple seeks to obey His "hard sayings," even when the full reason for them is not immediately evident, and even when it is not clear what "effectiveness" his obedience will have.
4. For Christ to be Lord means that His disciples take up "the cross." They follow His pattern of life and His verbal teachings in the renunciation of honor, wealth, security, falsehood, and violence.

C. The Holy Spirit makes real the life of Christ in the life of the believer.
1. To become a disciple of Christ can be spoken of as regeneration, new birth, or conversion: the gift of a new nature and will and direction.
2. The life of discipleship can be spoken of as sanctification, holiness, growth in conformity to His nature and will.
3. To live as a disciple demands a continuing recognition of one's own inadequacy: "yieldedness" in continuing recognition of one's need for grace. The believer confesses that need and renews his commitment to obedience.

D. The disciple of Jesus Christ is, like his Master, the servant of his neighbor.
1. The servant is guided by the need of the neighbor.
2. Cultural activity is not for selfish enjoyment or an end in itself, but for God and the neighbor.
3. Self-giving suffering love is at the heart of service. The way of the cross is the alternative to lordship (nonresistance).
4. The servant serves his neighbor by transparency and truth, by telling rather than by manipulating. (The rejection of the oath.)

IV. The mission of the church
A. The church is dispersed.
1. The church is cosmopolitan rather than being identified with

provincial interests, yet the local congregation seeks to be relevant and understood in its own situation.

2. The concern of the church is cosmic: every area of creativity belongs to her mission in the world.

3. The Christian is a pilgrim: he does not attach himself permanently to any place or culture; he lives in a voluntary minority community in a pluralistic society, in several overlapping communities or "worlds."

4. The church prays for all men that obedience to the will of God may increase.

B. In the midst of the world, the church as the first fruits of the new humanity is different from the world.

1. The uniqueness of the church will show in creativity in finding new ways of meeting needs, in "pilot" service to the larger society.

2. The church discerns and judges idolatry. She seeks to bring every kind of mental perception into subjection to Christ.

3. The church does not seek nor share sovereignty in the wielding of the sword among men.

4. Through her obedience to Christ the church testifies to the world concerning the meaning of His call.

C. The church calls men to response.

1. The message is not herself, but the heralding of the good news that God loves men and gave His Son for them.

2. She calls individual men to repentance and faith and to enter her new community.

3. She calls men to bring forth fruits worthy of repentance.

4. This call must be communicated in many ways; in words and deeds, in formal preaching and teaching, in unplanned questions and comments and fitting silences, in prophetic witness and in communal solidarity.

D. The church discerns the meaning of what God is doing in history.

1. She discerns His work of warning and judgment against idolatry and brutality and pride.

2. In performing the tasks described above she discerns the possibilities of building a relatively better order of society and calls upon men within the institutions of society to lead and modify these institutions in the interest of the welfare of man and in line with the divine standards of human welfare.

3. At the same time, she denounces the pretensions of men

that their social achievements, even if they be "relatively better," can be identified with God's righteousness and recognizes that God calls on all to repent and experience His renewing grace and transforming power in Christ.

4. She recognizes that what God is doing in history will culminate in a new heaven and new earth of God's own creation, and that all men are subject to final judgment.

V. Supplementary Statement on Childhood and Personhood

A. The question to which this statement seeks to speak

1. The cultural stream which we refer to as humanism has ever since the Renaissance augmented in many ways the weight of the concept of the individual "self" as a focus of values and duties.

2. Many developments arising out of the study and management of educational processes, and from psychology, have led to understandings of learning and growth as gradual, progressive, with no clear lines between childhood and adulthood.

3. Developments in religious education (of many different types, including "child evangelism") have underlined how widely the young mind may be influenced, and what a variety of "religious experiences" young persons are capable of under certain circumstances.

4. Developments in Mennonite self-understanding, by lifting up the "believers' church" character of the Anabaptist church type, have raised questions about the ways in which revivalism and child evangelism have tended to lower the age of baptism. These and other considerations called forth the decision, in the 1968 workshop, to assign for drafting two topics in this realm: one on the self and self-fulfillment, and another on the nurture and the religious experience of the child. This draft now attempts to speak to both of those areas, since they are closely connected.

B. The form of this outline

1. At some points, guidance will be taken, or precedents will be found, in certain traditional Anabaptist or Mennonite concepts.

2. The major headings of this supplement to the "theological statements" will be borrowed from the prior outline.

C. Since faith sees God as working in history to call into being a believing people,

1. We should not be attached to any definition of the "nature" of the human person as being static, but should welcome those

views of man's nature which see him as growing, as changing, as produced by his history (and as producing his history). These changing views of man's nature are interpreted in light of the biblical position that man is morally inadequate, even rebellious.

2. God's saving purpose for the individual should not be limited to to the "imputing" of a saved "status"; it must also be conceived as a call into a process, an experience, a growth, a social involvement.

3. The same must be said of lostness, which is not only a destiny of ultimate separation from God but also, already in this life, a process, a rebellion, a social involvement, and a pattern of learnings.

4. The young person is thus to be seen as bearing potentiality for learning in either direction. In line with the Anabaptist rejection of the traditional doctrine of original sin, which linked sinfulness to procreation, and which seemed to make God responsible for evil, the child should not be seen as evil, with a will which needs to be "broken" by education. In line with the Anabaptist rejection of infant baptism, the child should not be seen as a young church member needing only to be sheltered from harmful influences. The human person is at all ages, in varying degrees, an arena where the awareness of self is born and cultivated in the context of choice between good and evil.

5. Apart from the call of God, man is in slavery to himself and to sin.

D. Since faith sees the church as a reconciled and reconciling community,

1. The individual must be understood as finding his true destiny not in heroic independence or autonomous self-fulfillment, but in self-forsaking, forgiving discovery of community, whose existence, and whose mission, are prior to his own.

E. Since membership is a matter of free "adult" decision,

1. No person may be assumed or presumed to be destined to membership. This is the meaning of the Anabaptist rejection of infant baptism.

2. The function of nurture in the believing family (and in its extension in formal schooling) is to enable, as much as possible, a responsible, mature, free, informed answer — be it affirmative or negative — to the call of God, rather than to avoid such

a choice or to predetermine that it shall necessarily be affirmative. A loving, faith-oriented environment may heighten the youth's awareness of Christian understandings, including the concept of his being a sinner and of Christ's forgiveness; but it may also heighten his knowledge of the demands of discipleship and his capacity to ward off his community's pressures upon him. There should be no assumption that the believer's children *must* become believers.

3. No judgment should be assumed with regard to the spiritual status of the young person before his clearly having made such a choice. This is the validity (whatever may be the theoretical shortcomings) of the traditional Mennonite concept of an age of accountability, prior to which children are not to be considered condemned. The numerous religious and moral experiences of which younger persons are capable may be fostered and respected without seeking to identify them as the commitment of Christian faith.

4. There is no one who is not called to this discipleship. This is the abiding validity of the Anabaptist denial of the concept limited atonement and of the Anabaptist insistence upon the missionary imperative. No concept of the duties of believers toward their own children may be permitted to modify the primacy of the call of all men. The children of believers are socially privileged in their access to the gospel; they are not theologically privileged either by corporate election or by baptismal regeneration.

5. Genuine human decision has about it elements of both gradual and rapid change. Concern for the authenticity of the choice forbids prescribing any age level or any one experiential pattern of conversion. The validity of the request for baptism is founded not in a particular sequence of emotional experiences but in a set of understandings and a direction of commitment. It should be followed by further growth in knowledge, self-knowledge, and commitment, which again may proceed both gradually and in new crisis experiences.

6. Man may choose to identify by faith with Christ and the church.°

° He does not choose to be a sinner. He already is.

F. Since the disciple forsakes other values to follow Jesus Christ:
 1. The person who is ready for the decision to follow Christ is one who has some experiential awareness of the other claims upon his loyalty: "the world, the flesh, and the devil."
 2. The nurture of the children of believers should include a portrayal of those competing claims in their true light, but should not seek to "shield" the young person from the awareness of their attractiveness.
 3. Compliance with the call to discipleship is voluntary. The ethic of suffering servanthood can be imposed on no one. Genuine commitment to Christ cannot be "programmed." Respect for the reticence of the uncommitted is part of the love in which the call is proclaimed and a recognition of the danger of an inauthentic response.

G. Since the disciple confesses in Jesus Christ the model of true humanity to which all men are called:
 1. The call to love God and neighbor is addressed to all men; it is not a "special Christian ethic" irrelevant to unbelieving men, which it would be wrong to propose as a model to those who might choose not to believe.
 2. On the other hand, the call is not to "self-fulfillment" or personhood apart from Jesus Christ. Christians need to ward off the temptation to work with others (in family, school, or service agency) on the assumption that full, normal, decent human existence is a self-sufficient wholeness to which faith would be an optional additive.
 3. Nothing constitutive stands in the way of obedience to this call. This is the meaning of the Anabaptist rejection of the idea that original sin renders true belief and obedience impossible. The human person is seen as by grace capable of good; his disobedience is at least partly his own responsibility, and his repentance in the power of the Holy Spirit must be his own choice. We reject any views of "person" which make him the helpless object of forces beyond any control or the object of human control.
 4. The renunciation of self to which Jesus' disciples are called is ratified by the gift of the new selfhood: "he that loseth his life . . . shall find it." If Christians are embarrassed to call all men to that renunciation which is portrayed in the "hard words" of Jesus, they betray their own unbelief in His

promise. If they do not believe that the "strait and narrow way" is a gift of grace, that the call to "come and die" is a call to victory, they thereby reduce the gospel to a religiopsychological technique of self-starvation, and transform their own ethical earnestness into self-justification.

Appendix B

A Philosophy of Education
for the Mennonite Church:
Membership and Chronology

The preparation of this statement of educational philosophy has been carried out under the direction of the Philosophy of Christian Education Study Committee. This committee met first on March 5, 1966, and set the study in motion. The committee functioned primarily through a subcommittee, the Philosophy of Christian Education Research Committee. This subcommittee in turn assigned a part of its work to a group of six researchers who prepared a series of background reports. These reports are listed in the first section of the bibliography.

The names of the members of the Study Committee with the organizations they represent are given here, followed by the names of the Research Committee and the six researchers.

The Study Committee
Nelson E. Kauffman (chairman), Mennonite Board of Education
Daniel Hertzler (vice-chairman), Mennonite Publishing House
Dorsa J. Mishler (secretary), Mennonite Board of Missions
Paul M. Lederach, Mennonite Board of Education
Lloyd Weaver, Jr., Eastern Mennonite College Board of Trustees
Myron Augsburger, Eastern Mennonite College Board of Trustees
Ira E. Miller, Eastern Mennonite College
Orrin J. Smucker°, Lois Clemens°, Goshen College Overseers
Paul Mininger°, Carl Kreider°, Goshen College
Merle Bender°, J. N. Weaver°, Hesston College Overseers
Laban Peachey, Hesston College

64

Paul Yoder°, Levi Miller°, Secondary Education Council Administration
Don Augsburger, Secondary Education Council Board
J. Lester Brubaker°, Clarence Y. Fretz°, Association of Mennonite
Elementary Schools
Ross Bender, Mennonite Commission for Christian Education
Arnold Cressman, Mennonite Commission for Christian Education
Paul N. Kraybill°, Chester Wenger°, Eastern Mennonite Board of Missions
Virgil J. Brenneman, Student Services Committee

The Research Committee
Paul M. Lederach°, Daniel Hertzler°, chairman
Paul Bender, secretary
Don Augsburger
Melva Kauffman°, Laban Peachey°
Ira E. Miller
John Howard Yoder

The Researchers
(Titles of the six research papers appear below as the first section in the bibliography.)
J. Lester Brubaker, former Professor of Education, Eastern Mennonite College, now Superintendent of Lancaster (Pa.) Mennonite School.
Arnold Cressman, Field Secretary, Mennonite Commission for Christian Education.
Paul S. Kurtz, Professor of Psychology, Central Michigan University, Mt. Pleasant, Michigan.
Harold D. Lehman, Professor of Education, Madison College, Harrisonburg, Virginia.
Calvin Redekop, Professor of Sociology, Goshen College, Goshen, Indiana.
Paton Yoder, former Dean, Hesston College, Hesston, Kansas.

Additional Participants
By invitation of the Research Committee, the following persons participated in a four-day workshop on July 4-8, 1968, called for orientation of the six researchers. Thanks are due them for their interest and assistance.
Harold Bauman, Pastor to Students, Goshen College, Goshen, Indiana.

°More than one name indicates replacement during the period of study.

C. Norman Kraus, Chairman, the Division of Bible, Religion, and Philosophy, Goshen College, Goshen, Indiana.

Albert J. Meyer, Executive Secretary, Mennonite Board of Education.

Chronology of the Study

March 5, 1966. Organization of committee, appointment of Research Committee with Paul M. Lederach as chairman.

October 10, 1966. Proposed research design presented to Study Committee by Research Committee. Acceptance of proposal by Study Committee.

November, 1966. Resignation of Paul M. Lederach from Research Committee.

Spring, 1967. Appointment of Daniel Hertzler and Paul Bender to Research Committee as chairman and secretary.

September 18, 1967. Meeting of the Research Committee to clarify understanding of assignment and make plans to carry it out.

Spring, 1968. Circulation of a set of theological statements prepared by Paul M. Lederach and John Howard Yoder as foundation for Mennonite philosophy of education.

June 4-7, 1968. Workshop for orientation of six researchers. Participants included the six researchers, the Research Committee, and three additional invited persons mentioned above.

September 13-16, 1968. Workshop to receive reports of the six researchers and plan a report to the Study Committee.

October 7, 1968. Meeting of the Study Committee to receive the progress report of the Research Committee and assign further work.

January 6, 1969. Meeting of the Study Committee to approve plans for further activity of the Research Committee. Projects carried out during late 1968 and 1969 included a consultation on the question of psychology of learning, a mail consultation on the theological statements and interviews with selected Mennonite mission and relief administrators as "consumers" of Mennonite education. In the fall of 1969 and early 1970, attention was given to the drafting of a proposed statement of Mennonite philosophy of education as a report to the Study Committee.

May 7-9, 1970. Meeting of the Study Committee to receive and discuss the proposed philosophy statement. This was followed by revisions of the philosophy document in preparation for submission of a revised report to the Study Committee early in 1971.

Winter and spring, 1971. Revised report submitted to the Study Committee. Further revision and submission for publication.

Bibliographical Resources

No attempt has been made to provide a comprehensive bibliography in philosophy of education. Each of the materials listed here was simply found to have some bearing on the subject of the study. As will have been noted in reading the document, the contribution of some has been foundational while that of others is marginal.

Background Research Reports

The following research papers were prepared at the request of the Philosophy of Christian Education Research Committee as background material for the philosophy study. They were presented to the Research Committee during a four-day workshop held in September, 1968. Copies of these papers are available as long as the supply lasts in the office of the Mennonite Board of Education, 1700 S. Main St., Goshen, Ind. 46526.

Brubaker, J. Lester, "Current Philosphies of Education."

Cressman, Arnold, "Christian Education in the Congregation."

Kurtz, Paul S., "Personality Development and Learning Theory."

Lehman, Harold, "Survey of Educational Philosophies of Other Religious Groups Engaged in Elementary and Secondary Education."

Redekop, Calvin, "Mennonite Education and Social Change."

Yoder, Paton, "Toward a Mennonite Philosophy of Education Since 1890."

Books

Allport, Gordon W. *Personality and Social Encounter*. Boston: Beacon Press, 1960.

Augsburger, A. Don. *Creating Christian Personality*. Scottdale: Herald Press, 1966.

Barnett, Henlee H. *The New Theology and Morality*. Philadelphia: The Westminster Press, 1967.

Belth, Marc. *Education as a Discipline*. Boston: Allyn and Bacon, 1969.

Berkowitz, Leonard. *The Development of Motives and Values in the Child*. New York: Basic Books, Inc., 1964.

Blaine, Graham B., Jr. *Youth and the Hazards of Affluence*. New York: Harper and Row, 1966.

Blos, Peter. *On Adolescence, A Psychoanalytic Interpretation*. New York: The Free Press, 1962.

Boehlke, Robert R. *Theories of Learning in Christian Education*. Philadelphia: The Westminster Press, 1967.

Brown, William E. and Greeley, Andrew M. *Can Catholic Schools Survive?* New York: Sheed and Ward, 1970.

Cremin, Lawrence A. *The Genius of American Education*. Pittsburgh: University of Pittsburgh Press, 1965.

Erikson, Erik H. *Insight and Responsibility*. New York: W. W. Norton and Co., 1964.

Evans, Richard I. *B. F. Skinner. The Man and His Ideas*. New York: E. P. Dutton & Co., 1968.

Frankl, Viktor E. *Man's Search for Meaning*. New York: Washington Square Press, 1963.

Greeley, Andrew M., and Rossi, Peter H. *The Education of Catholic Americans*. Chicago: Aldine Publishing Co., 1966.

Green, Thomas F. "Education and Epistemology," *Faith-Learning Studies IV*. New York: Faculty Christian Fellowship, 1964.

Havice, Charles W. (Ed). *Campus Values*. New York: Charles Scribner's Sons, 1968.

Heath, Douglas H. *Why a Friends School?* Wallingford: Pendle Hill Publications, 1969.

Hilliard, F. H.; Lee, Desmond; Rupp, Gordon; Niblett, W. R. *Christianity in Education*. London: George Allen and Unwin, Ltd., 1966.

Homans, Peter (Ed.). *The Dialogue Between Theology and Psychology*. Chicago: The University of Chicago Press, 1968.

Hordern, William. *New Directions in Theology Today*. Vol I. Introduction. Philadelphia: The Westminster Press, 1966.

Janzen, Waldemar. *A Basic Educational Philosophy.* Winnipeg: Canadian Mennonite Bible College, 1966.

Lederach, Paul M. *Reshaping the Teaching Ministry.* Scottdale: Herald Press, 1968.

——————. *Mennonite Youth.* Scottdale: Herald Press, 1971.

Lidz, Theodore. *The Person: His Development Throughout the Life Cycle.* New York: Basic Books, 1968.

Little, Lawrence C. *Foundations for a Philosophy of Christian Education.* New York: Abingdon Press, 1962.

Lynn, Robert W. *Protestant Strategies in Education.* New York: Association Press, 1964.

Marty, Martin E. *The Search for a Usable Future.* New York: Harper & Row, 1969.

Morris, Colin. *Include Me Out.* Nashville: Abingdon Press, 1968.

Muirhead, Ian A. *Education in the New Testament.* New York: Association Press, 1965.

Nelson, C. Ellis. *Where Faith Begins.* Richmond: John Knox Press, 1967.

Pannenberg, Wolfhart. *What Is Man?* Philadelphia: Fortress Press, 1970.

Pattillo, Manning M., Jr., and Mackenzie, Donald M. *Church-Sponsored Higher Education in the United States.* Washington: American Council on Education, 1966.

Pierce, C. A. *Conscience in the New Testament.* Chicago: Alec R. Allenson, 1955.

Polanyi, Michael. *Personal Knowledge.* New York: Harper & Row, 1964.

Price, Kingsley. *Education and Philosophical Thought.* Boston: Allyn and Bacon, 1962.

Schramm, Wilbur. "The Nature of News" in Casty, Alan (Ed.). *Mass Media and Mass Man.* New York: Holt, Rinehart and Winston, 1968.

Slusser, Gerald. *A Dynamic Approach to Church Education.* Philadelphia: The Geneva Press, 1968.

Stinnette, Charles R., Jr. *Learning in Theological Perspective.* New York: Association Press, 1965.

Tournier, Paul. *A Place for You.* New York: Harper & Row, 1968.

Trueblood, D. Elton. *The Incendiary Fellowship.* New York: Harper & Row, 1967.

Yohn, David Waite. *The Contemporary Preacher and His Task.* Grand Rapids: William B. Eerdmans, 1969.

Articles and Related Materials

Alexander, Tom. "Psychologists Are Rediscovering the Mind." *Fortune.* 82:108 ff., November, 1970.

Augsburger, Myron. "The Renewal of Social Concern Among Evangelicals." Transcript of speech to Mennonite Central Committee Annual Meeting, January 23, 24, 1971.

Bloy, Myron B., Jr. "Culture and Counter-Culture." *Religious Education.* 54:357-362, September-October, 1969.

Fischer, John. "Survival University: Prospectus for a Really Relevant University." *Harpers.* 239:12-22, September, 1969.

—————. "Survival U Is Alive and Burgeoning in Green Bay, Wisconsin." *Harpers.* 242:20-27, February, 1971.

Gilbert, Richard R. "Sesame Street," *Presbyterian Life,* 23, 24:30-34, December 15, 1970-January 1, 1971.

Harris, Sydney J. "The Shell Game Called Tuition." *Chicago Daily News,* April 13, 1970.

Hostetler, John A. "Old Order Amish Child Rearing and Schooling Practices. A Summary Report." *Mennonite Quarterly Review.* 44: 181-191, April, 1970.

Klassen, Walter. "Conrad Grebel College Chapel" in *Annual Report, 1969.* Waterloo: Conrad Grebel College, 1969.

Kreider, Carl, "Becoming God's People Today — in Our World." Asdress at Annual Meeting, Mennonite Board of Missions, 1967.

Landry, Sabin P., Jr. "Some Reflections on State University Education in the 1970s." *Review and Expositor,* 67:17-30, Winter, 1970.

Loewen, Jacob A. "Socialization and Conversion in the Ongoing Church." *Practical Anthropology,* 16:1-17, January-February, 1969.

Meyer, Albert J. "Needed: A Mennonite Philosophy of Higher Education." *Mennonite Life,* 17:3, 4, January, 1962.

Miller, Donald E. "The Faith Community as Teacher." *Messenger,* 120: 23, 24, April 15, 1971.

Mininger, Paul. "Annual Report of the President." Goshen: Goshen College, 1961-62.

Ross, Albion. "The Small Religious College," *Center Magazine,* July, 1969.

Strommen, Merton P. "Alienation, Gratification and Disenchantment," *Religious Education,* 54:362-368.

Wenger, J. C. "How Do We Discover the Meaning of the Biblical Message?" Unpublished paper read to the Mennonite Publication Board in March, 1969.

Yoder, John Howard. "The Hermeneutics of the Anabaptists." *Mennonite Quarterly Review*. 41:291-308, October, 1967.

——————. "The Church and the World." Goshen: Goshen College Theological Workshop, 1958.

Zook, Ellrose D. *Mennonite Yearbook and Directory*. 62:16-21, 45, 1971.